MOTORCYCLES

RACE CAR LEGENDS

C O L L E C T O R ' S   E D I T I O N

MOTORCYCLES

Jeff Savage

CHELSEA HOUSE
PUBLISHERS

A Haights Cross Communications Company ®

Philadelphia

Cover Photo: Ricky Carmichael gets blasted with sand by a rider he is about to lap at the June 13, 2004, AMA Chevrolet Motocross Championship race in Southwick, Massachusetts. The veteran racer from Havana, Florida, dominated the 250cc National and claimed the 99th victory of his career.

CHELSEA HOUSE PUBLISHERS

VP, NEW PRODUCT DEVELOPMENT   Sally Cheney
DIRECTOR OF PRODUCTION   Kim Shinners
CREATIVE MANAGER   Takeshi Takahashi
MANUFACTURING MANAGER   Diann Grasse

STAFF FOR MOTORCYCLES

EDITORIAL ASSISTANT Sarah Sharpless
PRODUCTION EDITOR Bonnie Cohen
PHOTO EDITOR Pat Holl
SERIES DESIGN AND LAYOUT Hierophant Publishing Services/EON PreMedia

Original edition first published in 1997.

http://www.chelseahouse.com

A Haights Cross Communications ◥ Company ®

First Printing

1   3   5   7   9   8   6   4   2

Library of Congress Cataloging-in-Publication Data

Savage, Jeff.
   Motorcycles / Jeff Savage.
      p. cm.—(Race car legends. Collector's edition)
   Includes bibliographical references and index.
   ISBN 0-7910-8695-X
   1. Motorcycles, Racing–Juvenile literature. I. Title. II. Series.
GV1060.S28 2005
796.7'5–dc22

                                                    2005010504

All links and Web addresses were checked and verified to be correct at the time of publication. Because of the dynamic nature of the Web, some addresses and links may have changed since publication and may no longer be valid.

TABLE OF CONTENTS

RETURN OF THE KING

Jeremy McGrath sat in front of a microphone at Angels Stadium in Southern California, crying. It was January 2003, and McGrath was announcing his **retirement**. McGrath was the best rider in Supercross history. He had won more races and titles than anyone else. He was known simply as "The King of Supercross." Bob Hannah had won three straight **American Motorcyclist Association** Supercross Series championships in the 1970s. McGrath broke Hannah's record in 1996 by winning his fourth straight title. He would have won eight straight, if not for a second-place finish in the middle of the streak. But in 2001, McGrath began finishing behind other riders. The following year, he did not place in the top three until the season's eighth race. He was a fierce competitor, and the losing ate at him. His body was tired and his mind was worn out. He knew it as time to let go.

McGrath sobbed as he spoke. Hundreds of reporters, sponsors, riders, and others from the racing world cried along with him. "My recent injuries have played an important role in my decision to retire," Jeremy said slowly. "Time has also played an equally important role. . . . It kills me to be out there and not winning. I promised myself that when I wasn't 100 percent focused and motivated, it was time to

Jeremy McGrath powers through a turn during the 250-cc main event at the THQ AMA Supercross San Diego, that was held at the Qualcomm Stadium on February 19, 2005.

step down—and it is important to me to keep that promise to myself."[1]

Two years later, in February 2005, McGrath was at Angels Stadium again. This time, he was sitting on his red Honda 250 motorcycle at the starting gate. Nineteen other riders were lined up with him. McGrath leaned forward, keeping his front end tucked down, eyes pinned to the gate. At the drop, he grabbed a handful of throttle, and his bike snapped off the line. In the critical chase to the **holeshot**, where the order of the race is established, five riders beat him to it, and so he swept around the first turn in sixth place.

What was McGrath doing? He was "un-retiring." After two years away from the sport, he couldn't stand being away. He missed the exhaust. The dust. Most of all, he missed the competition. For McGrath, the only thing worse than not winning was not trying. This was the fifth round of the 2005 THQ American Motorcyclist Association (AMA) Supercross Series season. Two of the first four races were staged at Angels Stadium in Anaheim. McGrath competed in both. In the first, he crashed. In the second, he finished fifth. This would be the final event at this venue, before the series headed east. McGrath did not plan to compete in all the events. But he had to be here, a short drive from his home in Encinitas. "I'm realistic about this," McGrath said. "I'm not calling it a comeback. It's just that I want to race and want to have fun. It's never going to be like it was."[2]

Midway through the first of 20 laps, McGrath was chasing, in order: Michael Byrne, Ricky Carmichael, Erick Vallejo, Ernesto Fonseca, and Travis Preston. That order was about to change. Carmichael had been the primary reason McGrath stopped winning races. The 5-foot, 5-inch spark-plug racer from Florida had dominated the Supercross scene with three straight series titles until sitting out the previous season recovering from knee surgery. Carmichael was back in force in 2005, seeking his fourth straight win of the early season, and he showed it with a slick inside move around Byrne through a **hairpin** turn to take the lead at the end of

A group of competitors charge off the start line during the THQ AMA Supercross at Angels Stadium in Anaheim, California, on February 5, 2005.

the first lap. He increased his pace, stretched out his lead, and watched the other riders disappear. The battle would be for second place.

Meanwhile, McGrath was tearing it up, too. He skidded around a turn, his knobby rear tire spraying a rooster tail of dirt in the air, and then he gunned it down the straightaway at 70 miles per hour. He skipped through the **whoops** and muscled past Preston to move up to fifth. Moments later, he was overtaking Vallejo. Now he was running in fourth place. His desire was intense. He wanted more. It was just like old times. High over the track's big triple jumps he flew, and now he was right on the back bumper of Fonseca. The first three riders to finish a race are awarded prizes on the **podium**, and the sold-out crowd of 45,050 imagined their local hero standing there. ESPN2 announcer Todd Harris had it right when he said: "I guarantee you, if McGrath gets on the podium, Angels Stadium will absolutely erupt!"[3]

Riders call it dogging. It's when one rider is right behind another and threatening to pass at any moment. It happens in all motorcycle races, on the natural terrain of motocross tracks, on the pavement in hyper-speed Superbike road racing, and in the elbow-to-elbow battles of dirt track racing. It happens in Supercross, too, and it was happening right now to Ernesto Fonseca. McGrath had overtaken hundreds of riders through his career. It was such a natural maneuver to him that he could almost do it in his sleep. But as he came up on the heels of Fonseca, poised to take third place, something went terribly wrong. In his haste, McGrath had skipped through the tricky **rhythm section** with too much speed, and his front tire caught a bump. He lost control instantly. The jolt tossed him over the handlebars hard onto the ground. Fonseca escaped. For an instant, McGrath lay curled up in the dirt. And in the next breath, Vallejo roared past him on the left, followed by Preston and David Vuillemin on the right. McGrath staggered to his feet and stumbled a few steps to a stack of protective padding, where he slumped back to the ground. Just then, race officials were over him waving **yellow caution flags**, as doctors were helping him to his feet. He was not seriously injured—just bumps and bruises. Mostly, he suffered from a wounded pride.

Carmichael finished first by 20 seconds, followed by Chad Reed and Michael Byrne. McGrath placed 19th. He would have finished last if Kevin Windham hadn't been knocked from the race moments before his crash. Those seven Supercross championships seemed so long ago now.

Before McGrath ever started racing motorcycles, riders had been competing for a century. They raced on dirt, sand, mud, in sunshine and hailstorms, by stadium lights and candlelight. And they won aboard all manner of motorcycle machines. These winners all shared something in common, something beyond a love of winning. They shared a love of racing. This is the attitude that has always defined great motorcycle racers—the desire to compete, even when it appears from all sides that winning might be out of reach. It is the attitude that still grips Jeremy McGrath.

DID YOU KNOW?

Motorcycle engines are powered by gasoline fuel. Riders control the speed of the motorcycle by twisting the throttle on the right handlebar. The amount of twist determines the amount of gasoline sent to the engine. The fuel mixes with air as it enters the cylinder of the engine. The cylinder is shaped like a can. Motorcycles have from one to four cylinders. Inside the cylinder is a piston. Each movement of the piston is called a stroke. Smaller motorcycles have two-stroke engines. Bigger motorcycles have four-stroke engines. Fuel ignites on every second stroke in a two-stroke engine. Fuel ignites on every fourth stroke in a four-stroke engine. The piston moves down to allow air and fuel to enter the cylinder. Then the piston moves up and compresses the air and fuel. A spark plug ignites the mixture to cause combustion. The mixture is released from the cylinder in the form of exhaust.

②

EARLY DAYS

No single individual is credited with inventing the motorcycle. The basics of the machine as we know it today—a gas-burning engine between two same-size wheels—took form over several years in the late 1800s through the work of a number of men in Germany.

In 1876, Nikolaus Otto built an internal combustion engine. A year later, Dugald Clerk invented a **two-stroke** compression engine. In 1883, Gottlieb Daimler and Wilhelm Maybach produced a **four-stroke** gas engine, a model for the common motorcycle engine. At first, these engineers could not agree on where to attach the engine onto the vehicle. They even tried putting it behind the vehicle on its own little wheel.

In 1885, Karl Benz developed a three-wheel vehicle powered by a single-cylinder engine that he put under the seat. Later that year, Gottlieb Daimler designed a two-wheel machine with a wooden frame and iron tires. He attached the engine between the tires and called this boneshaker the *Einspur*, meaning "one-track." (In 1928, Benz merged his company with Daimler to form Daimler-Benz AG, which today manufactures the Mercedes-Benz automobile.)

Today, some consider Otto the chief inventor of the motorcycle because he spurred its creation by designing the internal

Gottlieb Daimler constructed the *Einspur*, or "one track," by mounting an engine between iron wheels that were attached to a wooden frame. Its construction ensured the ride would be a bone rattling experience.

combustion engine. Others give Daimler the lion's share of the credit because he came up with the basic two-wheel design. In either case, the motorcycle had been born.

On November 10, 1885, Paul Daimler, the engineer's 17-year-old son, climbed aboard the crude machine and rode uninterrupted from just outside Stuttgart, Germany, to a small village nearly four miles away. This maiden voyage inspired hope for a new form of personal transport. A rush of German engineers, along with others in France and England, joined in the pursuit to perfect the revolutionary vehicle. Most people saw this machine simply for what it was—a bicycle with a motor attached under the seat. The words motor and bicycle were thus combined to form the word motorcycle.

Motorcycle factories emerged in the industrial areas of Europe as manufacturers started producing scores of the two-wheel vehicles. Improvements were constantly being made, such as two-speed **transmissions** and air-cooled engines, but complaints from new owners poured in over the limitations of the machine. The best vehicles, like those produced by Germany's big motorcycle company owned by Heinrich Hildebrand and Alois Wolfmuller, were capable of moving at speeds up to 28 miles per hour, but they were difficult to start and often stalled. The company Hildebrand and Wolfmuller, started in 1894, collapsed after three years because so many owners demanded their money back.

That same year in France, Michel and Eugene Werner unveiled a machine on the streets of Paris with the engine above the front wheel. The Werner *Motocyclette* became an instant success and soon the Werners had a factory in London. A dozen *Motocyclettes* were sold in 1897, 300 the following year, and 1,000 three years later.

The United States entered the fray in 1900 when bicycle manufacturer Albert Pope fitted an engine to one of his bikes. A year later, George Hendee fastened a single-cylinder engine built by Swedish immigrant Carl Hedstrom to an Indian bicycle frame. When the motorized bicycle worked as hoped, the Indian Bicycle Company in Milwaukee, Wisconsin, immediately converted a major section of its factory to a motorcycle plant. In 1901, three Indian motorcycles were sold. Nearly 150 were sold the following year.

In 1901, designers William Harley and Arthur Davidson decided to team up to produce a motorcycle. They worked in secret in a 10- by 15-foot wooden shed in Davidson's backyard in Milwaukee and emerged four years later with a vehicle that would launch the new Harley-Davidson company to greatness.

Walter Davidson, first president of the Harley-Davidson Motor Company, poses with his bike after winning the 1908 Federation of American Motorcyclists' endurance run. He proved that American-made bikes were equal or superior to European-made bikes.

In 1906, the partners built and sold 50 motorcycles. The next year, they sold 150.

The two American companies tried to keep pace with the demand for motorized bikes, but by now thousands of motorcycles were being imported from France, Britain, and Germany, and being driven on America's roads. Enthusiasts were curious about how the new Harley-Davidson machine would compare to the European competition. They found out in June 1908 when Walter Davidson showed up on a Harley-Davidson bike at the starting line for the grueling Federation of American Motorcyclists' endurance run in the Catskill Mountains of New York.

By the end of the first day of the two-day event, 15 of the 61 riders had dropped out, but Davidson's machine was still going strong. He moved well ahead of the field the second day, traveling 180 miles around Long Island to Brooklyn to win the event in record time. A week later, Davidson set another record on his Harley-Davidson by traveling 50 miles of hilly terrain on Long Island on one quart and one ounce of fuel—the equivalent of 188 miles per gallon. These feats convinced the American public of the value of Harley-Davidson motorcycles, and within a decade, the Harley-Davidson partnership was building and selling 18,000 motorcycles yearly.

Back in Europe, racing motorcycles had become a popular—and often dangerous—sport. It began in 1897 with long-distance races across the continent involving both motorcycles and huge motorcars. A Frenchman named M. Bucquet dominated these events on his Werner motorcycle, winning the famed Paris-to-Vienna race in 1903 in record time. He was leading the Paris-to-Madrid sprint as well, traveling at a speed of almost 40 miles per hour, when the race was halted at Bordeaux, France. The motorcycles and oversized motorcars roaring together down the dirt roads created a dangerous combination of speed and metal, and overflow crowds that lined the route were in obvious jeopardy. Frenzied spectators often foolishly stepped forward into the road to get a closer look through giant dust clouds at oncoming vehicles. Several people died tragically each year, and with more than three million spectators cramming the Paris-to-Madrid route near Bordeaux and a number of careless observers already having been killed, the event was terminated. Races across the continent were never run again.

With the ill-fated marathons a thing of the past, the *Motorcycle-Club de France* sponsored a different type of race in 1904—a contest involving motorcycles only, and on closed roads. Teams of three riders representing five countries—Denmark, Great Britain, Germany, Austria, and France—competed in what organizers called the first International Cup Race. But the contest was sheer chaos from the start. Riders used motorcycles heavier than the declared weight limit of 110 pounds. Illegal engine parts were discovered on some of the vehicles. Sections of the road were even discovered to have been sprinkled with nails. The British team had so many tire punctures it was forced out of the race early. The ensuing outcry forced organizers to hide the race results from the public. It also led to the immediate formation of the *Federation Internationale de Motocyclisme* (International Motorcycling Federation) as the governing body for all European motorcycle events.

A second International Cup Race was run the following year with the same rules, but under more honest conditions, and only two riders out of 15 managed to finish the race with Herr Wondrick of Austria winning the 168-mile event at an average speed of 54.5 miles an hour. The third International Cup Race was held in 1906, this time in Austria, and it proved to be the last. With competitors yearning to ride bigger, more powerful machines, and organizers holding fast to the 110-pound limit, the event was discontinued. The International Cup Races stand as the first official motorcycle races in the history of the sport.

On May 27, 1907, 25 men and their motorcycles gathered in the chilly drizzle at a schoolhouse on the Isle of Man to make history. The Isle of Man is a tiny island of the British Isles in the Irish Sea. The men had come to compete in what today is widely considered the most famous motorcycle race ever—the Tourist Trophy Races. The TT Races, as they are commonly known, have featured the greatest racers the sport has to offer, and they are still quite popular today.

In 1907, the Auto Cycle Club of Britain established the Tourist Trophy Races on the Isle of Man. The club could not race in England because British authorities would not waive the 12 mile per hour speed limit for road races. This photo, taken in 1911, shows spectators gathered at a country crossroad to watch the race. Charlie Collier, who won the first TT Race, is shown coming from behind.

The TT Races were established by the Auto Cycle Club of Britain on the Isle of Man because British authorities would not give in to the pleas of the Auto Cycle Club to temporarily waive its restrictive speed limit of 12 miles per hour to allow for road races. The Isle of Man imposed no speed limit on its roads, and the Isle's government welcomed the races.

The course was laid out in the form of a triangle measuring almost 16 miles. The race called for five laps, a 10-minute rest, and another five laps for a total of 158 miles. At the drop of a flag, the riders were off, some gunning their primitive engines to slowly pick up speed, some pedaling to keep up until their engines kicked in. Over the muddy, pot-holed roads they went, dodging mystified onlookers who got too close to the action and animals who wandered onto the road. Only 10 riders out of 25 who started the race managed to finish, and when it was over, Charlie Collier had claimed first place in 4 hours, 8 minutes, 8 seconds, with an average speed of 38 miles an hour. Collier was rewarded with a small cash prize and the three-foot tall Tourist Trophy, a silver figure of the ancient Roman god Mercury.

As word spread of the early TT Races, more motorcycle companies became involved, sending their latest innovations to the tiny island and hiring the best drivers to race them. In 1911, entries doubled from the previous year to 104, and the course route was altered to include a climb up the eastern face of 1,400-foot Snaefell Mountain. Cycles with new two-speed and three-speed gears now had the advantage, and it was Indian, the American company, that led the way. British riders Oscar Godfrey, C.B. Franklin, and A.J. Moorhouse powered their chain-driven Indian bikes up and down the rutted dirt roads to take the first three places. The TT Races had by now become a famous tourist attraction, and despite an interruption by World War I they remained the most popular races in the world.

Meanwhile, British authorities held fast to their insistence that no public roads be used for racing, even once a year for a few hours. This frustrated British motorcycle companies such as Raleigh, Matchless, Triumph, and Royal Enfield as they watched the rise of other European companies as well as Indian and Harley-Davidson of the United States. In order to road-test their own machines, British manufacturers were forced to build not only motorcycles, but private race tracks as well. The most famous of these would be Brooklands. Built in 1907 in Surrey, England, Brooklands was the world's first artificially constructed race track. For the next 30 years, high-speed testing and hundreds of races took place on the 2.7-mile banked concrete oval. Not coincidentally, the British motorcycle industry boomed during this time.

Will Cook won the first official motorcycle race at Brooklands in April 1908, averaging 63 miles per hour on an NLG Peugeot. Six months later, Charlie Collier broke the world one-hour record astride a JAP Matchless by traveling 70 miles, 105 yards on the concrete track. Rider teams from Cambridge and Oxford Universities began a motorcycle competition a year later. And then, in 1911, one of the first-ever classic motorcycle races was staged. An overflow crowd of 35,000 turned out on a rare sunny day to see local countryman Charlie Collier go head-to-head with American Jake de Rosier. The program called for three races of two, five, and ten laps. Collier competed on a British-built red Matchless vehicle, de Rosier on a black chain-driven Indian machine with wide handlebars.

Collier grabbed the lead in the first race, but de Rosier pulled even down the first straightaway. Together they went up the Byfleet Banking, along the grandstand, and under Member's Bridge until de Rosier slowed and slipped in behind Collier. The British crowd cheered as Collier held the lead into the second lap, but it didn't know de Rosier's intent was to trail his opponent until the final moment. By allowing Collier to ride directly in front of him, de Rosier was using his opponent as a wind shield, a novel racing technique known as **slipstreaming**. As the finish line neared, de Rosier

Britain's ban on road racing led to the construction of private race tracks. Featured here is Brooklands, the most famous track, located in Surrey, England. Hundreds of races and speed trials took place at Brooklands until the site was converted to an aircraft factory at the outbreak of World War II. The track's popularity spurred a boom in motorcycle manufacturing.

pulled out from behind Collier at the final instant and roared past at 80 miles an hour to win by a split second.

Collier assumed the lead again in the second race, with de Rosier purposely "dogging" him from behind. It stayed that way until the end of lap three when de Rosier's motorcycle inexplicably took to lurching about the track. The American rider tried to maintain balance, but on the final lap his machine shook violently and then careened completely off the track and out of sight. Collier crossed the finish line alone. Moments later, de Rosier reappeared on the track to the cheers of the gracious crowd, wobbling toward the finish with a blown front tire.

The deciding 10-lap race was a back-and-forth battle early on as the riders exchanged the lead several times. Collier seized the lead around the high banking on lap five to the delight of the partisan spectators, but again, de Rosier was simply employing a tactical move to slipstream his opponent. One lap later, Collier's machine incurred minor engine trouble, and de Rosier blew on by. Collier made the necessary repairs on the move, and set out for the leader at full throttle, but de Rosier was too far ahead and could not be caught; de Rosier had recorded a historic victory at Brooklands and given the Indian company and all America cause to celebrate.

Brooklands would play host to many more great races. But at the outbreak of World War II, the oval course had to be converted to a site for an aircraft factory. Racing would never return to Surrey.

One of the most dangerous enduro races is the Paris - Dakar Rally. It is a two-week race that starts in Paris, France and extends through vast stretches of African desert before ending in Dakar, the capital of Senegal. There are divisions for motorcycles, cars, and trucks.

In 2005, racers were reminded again of the dangers of the Paris-Dakar Rally. Two motorcyclists were killed in the race. First, a rider from Spain named Jose Manuel Perez died in the hospital following a crash. Then, Fabrizio Meoni of Italy died from a heart attack after a crash. Meoni, who had won the rally twice, had told other riders that this would be his last Paris-Dakar.

③
OFF-ROAD RACING

While speed had become glamorous, the handling of a motorcycle over rough terrain was a sight to be admired. Some enthusiasts even considered it to be pure art. The reliability of the machine, and the skill of the rider, were united by a new version of the sport called trials riding. It is the forerunner to today's **motocross** and **Supercross**.

In trials riding, a rider had to negotiate tricky natural hazards like rocks and boulders, sand and mud, fast-flowing streams, and near-vertical climbs and drops. Doing so required steady concentration, incredible balance, and a feeling of unity with the motorcycle.

The first trials competition, held in 1903 in London, was a 10-day affair, and everyone who finished received an award. The event was shortened to a single day the next year, and soon the rules were altered to allow spectators to follow the action more easily. The course was divided into short "sections" over which one rider at a time would travel. The rider was permitted to inspect the section before riding over it in order to plan his strategy. He then tried to carefully maneuver his motorcycle over and around obstacles without stopping or putting a foot on the ground. Officials observed the action, and the rider lost one point for **dabbing**, or momentarily touching his foot to the ground to keep his balance, and five points for stopping or falling over. He was awarded a "clean" by completing the section without penalty. Riders developed techniques like standing high on their footpegs for balance or leaning rearward to put weight on their back tire for better traction. Two of the greatest trials riders in history were Ireland's Sammy Miller, who won five International Six-Days Trials and numerous other trials in the 1960s, and Finland's Vrjo Vesterinen, who won several world championships in the 1970s.

The most popular trials race is the International Six-Days Trial, which was started in 1913. It has grown to become one of today's most prestigious motorcycle events in the world. It lasts six days and is held in a different country each year. The winner is awarded the Premier World Trophy and the top four-man team receives the Silver Vase. The International Six-Days Trial is different from the early trials because it is based strictly on time. The course can run as long as 2,000 miles, and competitors race each day until a point in time at which they are halted and their bikes taken away and locked in storage for the night. The winner is the one who crosses the finish line first.

Because of its emphasis on time, the International Six-Days Trial is really is more of an enduro event. Enduro races are long-distance races that test the durability and endurance of riders and their motorcycles. Like trials riding, the enduro course is divided into sections. Riders are timed over each section and their standing is determined by their combined time.

Enduro courses often stretch across desolate terrain, and riders are required to make their own repairs. They carry tools that fit every nut and bolt on their machine, along with spare parts, and sometimes even a backup electrical system and spare tire. The two most popular enduro races today are

The International Six Days Trial is an enduro event that is held in a different country each year. A motorcycle racer with sidecar is shown stuggling up the hill during the Auto Cycle Union Six Day Trials at Buxton, England, in 1926.

the Baja 1000 through the dust and sandy terrain in Mexico, and the Paris-Dakar rally, which runs from France to Africa and takes nearly three weeks to complete.

In the 1920s, the Tourist Trophy Races were still going strong on the Isle of Man. Jimmy Simpson became the first rider to lap the course at 60, 70, then 80 miles an hour. Stanley Woods won his first TT Race in 1923 on his way to a record 10 victories. But off-road racing had become the rage in Europe, especially in Britain, and no version of the sport seized fans like the frenzied contest of scrambling.

Modern day enduro events, such as the "Enduro du Touquet," test the stamina of driver and machine. A crowded field of racers pass through the dunes section of the enduro on the beach of Le Touquet, in northern France, in February, 2001.

Rough Rider Scrambles first appeared in England in the early 1920s, and the first officially sanctioned competition took place in the town of Surrey in 1924. Scrambles were similar to trials racing, but without observed sections. Riders removed all unnecessary parts to make their motorcycles lighter—even tire guards and exhaust pipes. In that first official race, 80 riders battled on a 30-mile course over the roughest terrain possible and nearly half of them didn't finish.

The winner was A.B. Sparks aboard a Harley-Davidson. The hectic action that day was described by one of the race organizers as "a rare old scramble." That is how scrambling got its name, and it was not until two decades later that the sport became known as motocross.

As scrambling took hold in continental Europe, the French word motocyclette and the English term cross-country were combined to form the name motocross. The action was breathtaking, as riders flew with reckless abandon over ruts and jumps and elbowed one another in tight turns. But the riders were disappointed to find that rules at different tracks varied wildly to include such particulars as heats, time scales, and unlimited weight allowances and engine sizes. They demanded better-organized events with standard rules, and in 1947 the prestigious *Motocross des Nations* (Motocross of the Nations) was founded. A French businessman named Roland Poirer, who had been staging motocross events near Paris for several years, decided that year to bring together teams from Britain, France, Belgium, and Holland to compete in what he declared would be an annual competition between teams of riders from different nations. Each team consisted of five riders competing on 500-cc motorcycles (engine size is measured in cubic centimeters), and the team from Great Britain claimed the first-place prize. Thousands of fans embraced this spectacle, and motocross was soon flying high. It would not be long now until this thrilling sport reached the shores of the United States.

Teams from Great Britain and Belgium jockeyed for first place on the *Motocross des Nations* tracks and in the standings. Britain won three of the first five events, Belgium the other two, and then Britain won the next three. In 1955, the team from Sweden broke the streak, and for eight years,

Sweden and Britain traded victories, each winning four titles. The arrival of Jeff Smith secured Britain's high standing for several more years.

Smith entered his first motocross race in 1951, and he recalled that there were three people in the race and he finished third. However, he developed his racing skills in trials riding on the desolate Yorkshire moors, and he put BSA on the map as a producer of fast, reliable scramblers when he won the British championship in 1953 and 1954. Riding for his home country in the *Motocross des Nations*, Smith led Britain to five straight titles from 1963 to 1967. Smith's streak ended in 1968 when Russia captured the trophy.

The following year marked the arrival of the great Roger de Coster, a daring rider from Belgium who signed a lucrative deal with Suzuki, triggering a Japanese advance into motorcycle manufacturing that would lead to dominance in the world market by the "Big Four"—Honda, Kawasaki, Yamaha, and Suzuki. Over the next 11 years, de Coster led Belgium to six *Motocross des Nations* titles. Back in 1957, a motocross world championship series was devised in which riders accumulated points based on their finish at various events throughout Europe. With his knack for claiming the holeshot—getting to the first turn in front—and thereby leaving the rest of the field to battle for position in the spraying mud, de Coster captured the World Championship title three straight years, from 1971 to 1973. His streak was snapped in 1974 by Finland's Heikki Mikkola, a soft-spoken rider known by his legion of fans as the Flying Finn. Mikkola captured the title astride his Swedish-built Husqvarna. de Coster finished second in the standings, and then went to the United States to win the Trans-AMA motocross title, the forerunner to the AMA National Championship Series. de Coster regained the World Championship title in

Renown Belgian racer, Roger de Coster, won six *Motocross des Nations* titles, and triggered the Japanese advance into motorcycle manufacturing when he signed a lucrative deal with Suzuki.

1975, and he won it again in 1976. Meanwhile, he had shown Americans the best the world had to offer in motocross, and it was a challenge the U.S. riders were ready to meet.

In 1971, the first official motocross was held in the United States when the American Motorcyclists Association hosted an event on a temporary track at Daytona International Speedway in Florida. A year later, another motocross was held at Daytona, but this time inside the stadium. This event was unique because stands surrounded the track, which allowed spectators to view the entire competition. Organizers immediately dubbed it "Supercross." Jim Weinert of Middletown, New York, cruised to victory aboard his Yamaha. But it wasn't until an event later that year that this new version of motocross gained worldwide attention.

On July 8, 1972, more than 35,000 people poured into the Los Angeles Memorial Coliseum to see how the American riders compared to the best in the world. The Americans had challenged the Europeans to a Supercross race. The program called for a three-race competition in which points were awarded for each race based on order of finish. The rider who amassed the most points would be declared the overall winner. Three times, 20 riders shot from the gate at once and powered down the track. Into steep banked turns, called berms, they went, through the little kicker bumps on the straightaway, over the double and triple jumps they flew. When the last race was run and the dust had settled, three riders from Sweden—Torlief Hansen, Arne Kring, and Haken Andersson—had taken the checkered flag in the three races. But none of these riders was the overall champion. That honor went to little-known Marty Tripes of Santee, California. Tripes performed solid maneuvers all day on his Yamaha to finish second in all three races. Such consistency earned him all the points he needed to capture the overall title. Even more amazing, Tripes was only 16 years old and this was his first competition ever.

That same year, the AMA established a formal National Championship Series for both motocross and Supercross, much like the World Championship series in Europe. Two classes were established in motocross—a 250-cc class and a bigger 500-cc class. Supercross had a single 250-cc class. Riders accumulated points at each race based on their placement, and overall champions were declared. In the 500-cc motocross series, 18 races were held from April to December. The first two events, at Atlanta, Georgia, and Memphis, Tennessee, were won by the same rider—Barry Higgins, of Schenectady, New York. Then a brash young rider named

Brad Lackey took the American motocross world by storm. Lackey, from the tiny town of Pinole, in northern California, was a fearless rider who was known for his bold passing moves that sometimes seemed to defy gravity. Lackey roared to victory aboard his Kawasaki in 12 of the final 16 events. He accumulated 2,030 points, more than twice that of the next rider, Gary Jones of Hacienda Heights, California.

The Europeans preferred the World Championship series events on their own continent, but they proved their world-wide dominance in the sport when a single European, Pierre Karsmakers from Holland, came to the United States in 1973 to try his skill on the AMA 500-cc circuit. Karsmakers wound up winning 14 of the 23 events on his Yamaha to rack up 2,659 points, breaking Jones's record. A host of Americans were left to battle for second place. The same sort of skills— strength, balance, and ultra-quick reactions—required in motocross are used in Supercross as well. Karsmakers demonstrated as much when he entered the 250-cc Supercross series the following year and took that title, too.

Jim Weinert, the winner of the first AMA Supercross event at Daytona Beach, also proved that he could cross over, as he rose to the top of the motocross charts in 1974 by winning four straight 500-cc events and taking the overall title. Weinert had moved to Laguna Beach, California, to be closer to many of the events, and his dedication paid off with another championship trophy in the 500-cc class in 1975. He capped his racing career with a 250-cc Supercross title a year later.

Small 125-cc bikes were a third class added to the moto-cross competition, and Bob Hannah stormed onto the scene by winning five of the eight 125-cc events in 1976 to run away with the overall title. Hannah, like many racers, grew up in California, where he began riding motorcycles in vacant fields in his small hometown of Whittier. He came to be known as "Hurricane" Bob Hannah, and he proved his championship and his nickname worthy by dominating the Supercross scene the next three years, winning 18 events and claiming the points titles every time. Hannah won back-to-back titles at the 250-cc level in motocross in 1978 and 1979 as well.

The next great rider to emerge was Broc Glover, whose dexterity on the small bikes seemed almost unnatural. Glover, who liked to stand straight up over most of the course, learned to ride on dirt trails that wound through the eastern outskirts of El Cajon, California, just 15 miles north of Mexico. On August 14, 1977, in San Antonio, Texas, Glover needed a victory in the final race of the 125-cc season to tie Danny LaPorte in the points standings. LaPorte had won the first race of the series, Glover the fourth, and "Hurricane" Bob Hannah the other three. After Glover got his victory on a Yamaha, he and LaPorte finished the season tied with 240 points each, but Glover was awarded the points championship based on number of wins.

Glover left nothing to chance the following year, winning six of 10 races to claim his second points title. He outclassed the field again in 1979 by winning consecutive races in California, Arizona, Nebraska, and Texas, to breeze to his third straight points championship. Mark Barnett of Bridgeview, Illinois, won the last three events of the season, but Glover's points lead was well beyond reach by then.

Barnett came back to repeat his feat of three straight event wins to close the 1980 season, and this time his victories in Washington, New York, and Florida were enough to edge Glover, 314 to 309, for the overall points title. Glover moved up to the big bikes the following year, the 500-cc class, and he stunned the motorcycle world by immediately winning the first four events in Massachusetts, Pennsylvania, Florida, and Colorado. He won the final two events as well and easily captured the points title. Glover continued his motocross assault by taking the 1983 and 1985 points titles, his run interrupted only in 1984 when a young rider named David Bailey amazingly won the season's first eight races, leaving Glover to win the other two and settle for second place. Glover also won nine Supercross events in his career, but he never finished higher than second overall.

More stunning than Glover's 500-cc title in 1981 was America's performance that year at the *Motocross des Nations*. The United States had yet to win in the 34-year history of the famed event, though they had come close in recent attempts, finishing in the top 10 six straight times from 1972 to 1978 before not entering a team in 1979 and 1980. In 1974, the U.S. team of Jim Pomeroy, Brad Lackey, Tony DiStefano, and Jim Weinert finished second to a great Swedish team led by Haken Andersson and Arne Kring. In 1977, DiStefano was joined on the U.S. team by Kent Howerton, Gary Semics, and Steve Stackable, and together they pushed Belgium to the wire. But the Belgians, led by Roger de Coster, held off the Americans to claim the title.

In 1981, U.S. fortunes changed in a dramatic way. The foursome of Chuck Sun of Sherwood, Oregon, and three California riders, Johnny O'Mara of Van Nuys, Danny LaPorte of Yucca Valley, and Donnie Hansen of Simi Valley, captured the team title for the United States. All four were top-notch riders on the AMA circuits, and their victory was testimony to the skills of off-road racers in the United States. What's even more stunning is that this triumph would ignite a streak of 13 straight *Motocross des Nations* victories for the Americans, a run of dominance that may never again be matched. Twenty riders took part in the 13-year streak, led by Jeff Ward of San Juan Capistrano, California, who competed on seven of the championship teams, and David Bailey of Axton, Virginia, who competed on five.

Bailey burst onto the racing scene by winning the 1983 motocross and Supercross 250-cc points titles. He won the 500-cc motocross title in 1984, and again in 1986, and staged some of the best races the sport had to offer with new rival Rick Johnson. In one memorable Supercross race in 1986, over 71,000 fans at Anaheim Stadium in Southern California watched as Bailey and Johnson rode elbow-to-elbow nearly the entire way until Bailey surged ahead with three laps left. He crossed the line first, and then he collapsed from exhaustion. Twenty years later, many still consider this the greatest race in Supercross history.

Bailey's great career came crashing to a halt in January 1987, at a non-national race in Huron, California. Bailey didn't get his usual thrust off a triple jump, and he came up short, slamming into the third jump. He shattered his fifth vertebra on impact and severed his spinal cord. Today he is confined to a wheelchair, but ever the competitor, he now races the chair in events all across the United States.

Bailey's crash was an ugly accident for a sport that had been enjoying rising attendance for a decade and was just starting to reap the profits of television exposure. But like any motorsport, crashes are part of the business, and so sponsors remained loyal, and the industry pressed on.

Rick Johnson, Bailey's rival except when they teamed up for two *Motocross des Nations* championships, assumed command of the sport. Johnson won six points titles in the 250-cc and 500-cc classes in motocross and Supercross between 1986 and 1988. His record of 28 Supercross victories

Jeremy McGrath salutes fans while on the winner's stand at Anaheim Stadium. McGrath moved up to the 250-cc category and won ten events in the 16-event circuit at Anaheim, Seattle, San Diego, and Tampa. In 1993 he became the first rookie to win an AMA Supercross Championship series title.

aboard Honda bikes stood until 1995 when Jeremy McGrath, another Honda rider, blew past.

Like many Supercross riders, McGrath had grown up in Southern California where he learned to ride motorcycles at an early age. With the help of his father, he built a dirt track, complete with jumps, in a vacant field behind his house.

Jeremy would hurry home from school each day to ride on his track until it got dark or his bike ran out of gas. McGrath's ascension to the top of the Supercross world as the sport's all-time great was as fast and furious as his performances on the track. He had won the 125-cc Western Region Supercross Championship in 1991 and 1992, but when he moved up to the 250-cc class in 1993, people wondered whether he could handle the bigger bikes. He showed his strength from the outset, winning consecutive events at Anaheim, Seattle, San Diego, and Tampa. In all, he recorded a record 10 victories on the 16-event circuit to breeze to the points championship. He became the first rookie to win the series title. A star was born.

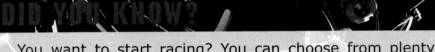

DID YOU KNOW?

You want to start racing? You can choose from plenty of events. The American Motorcyclist Association (AMA) sanctions 15 kinds of competition. Here is the list:

Motocross	Drag Racing
Arenacross	Dirt Drag
Dirt Track	Hillclimbs
Road Racing	Observed Trials
Enduros	Land Speed Record Trials
Hare Scrambles	Speedway
Hare and Hound	Ice Racing
Supermoto	

For a description of these competitions, you can go online to the AMA Racing website at *www.ama-cycles.com*.

McGrath won again in 1994, then tied Hannah's mark of three in a row the following year. In 1996, McGrath won his fourth straight points championship in convincing fashion, winning the first 13 races on the circuit before Jeff Emig broke the streak in St. Louis. McGrath crossed the line a wheel behind. "The moon, stars, and planets were all lined up perfectly for me," Emig said.[4]

McGrath's run of titles ended in 1997 when he finished second to Emig in the points standings. Emig was a veteran racer who had been named to the United States *Motocross des Nations* team five times and won it in 1995. This was Emig's first Supercross championship. McGrath made sure it was his only one. McGrath regained the title in 1998 and won it again in 1999. In 2000, McGrath won it for the seventh and final time.

McGrath's dominance left others to battle for second place. Mike LaRocco was a great racer whose only real record of note is most career second-place finishes. Mike Kiedrowski won four Motocross National Championships, but never a Supercross points title. "The MX Kied," as he was called, retired from competitive racing at the young age of 27. McGrath won the first of his record 72-career AMA Supercross victories in Anaheim. In 2001, he won his last race there, too. It came in an elbow-to-elbow battle with a brash newcomer named Ricky Carmichael. Before long, Carmichael was showing McGrath what it was like to eat dirt.

④ ON-TRACK RACING

While motocross and Supercross were dominating the off-road scene in the United States, two other forms of racing were flourishing on the track—road racing and dirt track racing.

In 1931, the AMA organized the first road races in the United States, and six years later, the first Daytona 200 was held in Florida. American road racing evolved from European Grand Prix racing, which had begun as long-distance contests over punishing roads but were shortened in the 1920s to races on paved circuits about five miles in length. The Belgian Grand Prix of 1921 is considered the first big continental race, and the French Grand Prix, which actually began a year earlier, has become the most famous.

Meanwhile, Daytona had been the premier site for car **drag races** and **land speed records**, and even a number of motorcycle speed records set mostly by Harley-Davidson machines. Ninety-eight riders entered the first Daytona 200 in 1937, which was held on a temporary beach course, where it would remain until after World War II. Ed Kretz of Pomona, California, won the inaugural race astride an Indian-built machine. Ben Campanale of Providence, Rhode Island, won the next two races on Harley-Davidson bikes; and Babe Tancrede of Woonsocket, Rhode Island, won in

Motorcycle racers are shown at the starting line at Daytona International Speedway. The first Daytona 200 was held on a temporary beach course in 1937. In 1961, the event moved to the newly paved Daytona Speedway. The track's enclosed race bowl design with its steep-banked turns enabled top speeds and instantly attracted worldwide attention.

1940, also on a Harley-Davidson. At the outbreak of World War II, racing in the United States and most of the rest of the world shut down and did not resume until 1946.

In 1949, Europe instituted the Road Racing World Championships, in which points were awarded at Grand Prix events, and a winner was declared at year's end. In the United States, a different points championship was about to be created. Dirt track racing on mile-long ovals was being contested at small tracks around the country, the most popular of which was the yearly battle at the Illinois State Fairgrounds which had begun in 1937 when Lester Hillbish of Reading, Pennsylvania, took the checkered flag. Indian motorcycles claimed the first five titles at the Springfield oval, and then Chet Dykgraaf of Grand Rapids, Michigan, broke the streak in 1946 on a Norton. An impressive young rider named Jimmy Chann, who grew up in Bridgeton, New Jersey, followed Dykgraaf with three straight victories aboard a Harley-Davidson. In 1954, the AMA established a points championship over 18 events called the Grand National Series. The granddaddy of these races was a 25-mile contest at the Illinois State Fairgrounds called the National Dirt Track Championship. In the inaugural year of 1954, Joe Leonard of San Jose, California, won eight events, including the prize race in Springfield, to run away with the points championship. Leonard's eight-victory season would stand as a record for 32 years.

Leonard won back-to-back points titles on a Harley-Davidson in 1956 and 1957, but this feat was immediately topped by Carroll Resweber of Cedarburg, Wisconsin, who claimed consecutive titles the next four years. Resweber edged Leonard by a point for his first title, and Leonard would claim runner-up status to Resweber twice more. Bart Markel of Flint, Michigan, would win the following year, and take two more titles aboard Harley-Davidsons in 1965 and 1966.

Speeds had now reached 100 miles an hour down the straightaways, and Japanese motorcycles were making huge inroads into the American market. Gary Nixon of Cockeysville, Maryland, won back-to-back points titles in 1967 and 1968, and daredevil Kenny Roberts of Modesto, California, aboard a Japanese-built Yamaha, took consecutive titles in 1973 and 1974.

Speed records were being broken everywhere. At the Tourist Trophy Races on the Isle of Man, Mike Hailwood of England celebrated his 10th year at the event in 1967 by averaging over

100 miles per hour on his Honda to win his 11th TT title, breaking the longstanding mark of Stanley Woods. Nicknamed "Mike the Bike," Hailwood went on to win a record 12 silver trophies. Speeds on the island track increased by the mid-1970s to 105 miles per hour or more, prompting such stars as Italy's Giacomo Agostini and England's Phil Read to complain that the course needed to be redesigned to accommodate such speeds.

Back on the Grand National Series circuit, Jay Springsteen of Lapeer, Michigan, powered his Harley-Davidson to three straight points championships from 1976 to 1978. Bubba Shobert of Lubbock, Texas, who doubled as a road racer, matched Springsteen's exploits on a Honda with three wins of his own from 1985 to 1987. In 1986, Shobert won the final event of the year in Sacramento, California, to finish with nine victories in the season, breaking Joe Leonard's longstanding record.

Meanwhile, American road racing had blossomed through sponsorships and television coverage. The biggest boost was triggered by Daytona. The event had been moved in 1961 to the recently paved Daytona International Speedway track operated by Bill France, a former stock-car driver. The impressive track immediately captured worldwide attention. Its design—an enclosed race bowl with 31-degree bankings at each end—allowed for top speeds. Also, the Daytona event kicked off the American road racing season each year, and so showcased the latest innovations by motorcycle manufacturers. In 1968, Cal Rayborn of San Diego, California, became the first rider in the history of the event to lap the entire field of riders and average over 100 miles an hour for the race. Rayborn won again on a Harley-Davidson the next year, and Dick Mann of Richmond, California, followed with consecutive victories, first on a Honda, then on a BSA.

In 1974, the 200-mile Daytona course was temporarily shortened to 180 miles because of the Middle East oil crisis. Giacomo Agostini, the great Italian record-breaker who would win an amazing 15 World Championships in Europe along with 10 Tourist Trophy Races, was one of 40 foreign entries that year. It was Agostini's first race on a Yamaha, and his first race in the United States. And he won it, recording an average speed of 105.01 miles per hour to set a Daytona record.

Kenny Roberts of Modesto, California, followed Agostini's victory at Daytona with four wins in the last five events on Yamaha-built bikes to win the 1974 points title. Three years later, Roberts won the newly-created **Superbike** points total in the **Formula One** category (500-cc engines), before leaving the United States to try his skill at the European circuit. He was an immediate success, becoming the first American to win a road racing World Championship in 1978. Roberts followed with another title in 1979.

In 1976, the AMA created a new version of road racing called the Superbike Series. Superbikes are modified versions of the big four-stroke machines that are sold for street use. They must have at least 650-cc engines, and they generally cost as much as a car. On March 5, 1976, the first AMA Superbike National was held at the steep-banked race bowl of Daytona. Steve McLauglin of Santa Ana, California, won the race on a BMW-built bike by the length of his front tire over Reg Pridmore of Goleta, California. Pridmore, who had moved to Southern California from England a decade earlier, came back to win the final two Superbike events of 1976 to claim the points title.

In 1977, there were seven Superbike events and seven different winners. Pridmore was one of the winners and also the most consistent, and so he captured his second straight

This scene from the 2002 World Superbike Championship race that took place in South Africa, shows how racers lean into the turns. A Superbike is a modified version of a street bike with at least a 650-cc engine. The first AMA Superbike race was held in 1976 at the Daytona International Speedway.

points title. He followed it with a final championship in 1978, when he was nearly 40 years old. He retired from racing the following year.

In 1984, a new Superbike star emerged as Fred Merkel set an AMA record with 10 victories on a Honda. Merkel grew up in Stockton, California, where he rode on dirt tracks as a boy before his father suggested that he switch to pavement. He joined the Superbike Series in 1983 and quickly earned the nickname "Flying Fred" because of his all-out assault on the tracks. Merkel won points titles three years in a row from 1984 to 1986, then he moved to Italy to race. In 1988, the world motorcycle governing body, *Federation Internationale de Motocyclisme* (FIM), established the World Superbike

Championships, and Merkel won the inaugural title. He came right back the following year to win the world title again. After being injured in an accident in 1995 at Firebird International Raceway in Arizona, Merkel retired from racing.

Bubba Shobert was already an accomplished dirt track racer when he tried road racing for the first time in 1984. He would become a Grand National Dirt Track champion three times over, but he also wanted to race motorcycles on the asphalt. On September 30, 1984, Shobert entered the Formula One event at the Mid-Ohio Sports Car Course in Lexington, Ohio. Skeptics said the kid from Lubbock, Texas, couldn't make the transition from dirt to pavement. To make matters worse, it rained all morning and throughout the race. Shobert won anyway. Some said it was because the track was slick and he was used to sliding around in the dirt on his motorcycle. Shobert knew otherwise. He had a winner's confidence, and the type of track didn't matter. In Shobert's first full year of Superbike competition, 1986, he finished in the top three at three events.

Shobert was originally from Lubbock, Texas, but he was living at the time in Carmel Valley, California, and in 1987 he won the Superbike event at the seaside oval in nearby Monterey. He wound up third in the overall points standings that year and vowed to do better. In 1988, Shobert won it all. He took first place at events in Georgia, Ohio, and Monterey again, and he edged fellow Texan Doug Polen to take the Superbike points total. In so doing, he became the first rider from outside California to win the points total in the 13-year history of the Superbike Series.

Shobert's hopes of defending his Superbike points total were tragically dashed at the first event of the 1989 season at Laguna Seca, California, when he slammed into the back of another rider who had stopped in the middle of the track at the end of the race to perform a trick. Shobert suffered severe head injuries. After hours of surgery, doctors saved his life, but he would never race again.

A wildly popular motorcycle event is **Freestyle Motocross** (FMX). It was introduced at the 1999 X Games. Riders go as high as possible on a 250-cc bike, pull off a trick in midair, and then try to land as safely as possible. In an FMX event, each rider gets two 60-second runs. Judges score each performance on overall impression, tricks, execution, use of the course, and landings. Travis Pastrana is known as "Wonder Boy" for his FMX acrobatics. Pastrana won the 1999 event, then won again the following year.

In 2001, a second motorcycle event called Big Air was introduced at the X Games. It involves a single jump off a ramp, encouraging riders to put all their effort into their biggest trick. Carey Hart attempted a back flip called "The Hart Braker." Hart had failed in his first attempt a year earlier at another event called the Gravity Games. At the X Games, Hart launched straight up, then yanked the handlebars. Suddenly, the 212-pound motorcycle was over his head. While inverted, he lost his grip with his right hand. He went into a freefall. His body slammed to the ground. Doctors and race officials were with him in an instant. After 10 minutes, they carried him to a waiting ambulance. Hart had suffered broken ribs and feet.

A third motorcycle event introduced at the X Games is called Step-Up. It is similar to the high jump in track and field. Riders soar high to clear a pole above the track. At the 2004 X Games, Jeremy McGrath was invited for the first time to compete in the Step-Up, and he won the event at a height of 32 feet, 6 inches.

Other racers have been more fortunate following crashes. Miguel Duhamel crashed in each of the first two Superbike events of 1995, at Daytona International Speedway and the Pomona Fairplex in Southern California, yet his padded racing outfit and Kevlar helmet saved him from injury. Duhamel took third place at Laguna Seca Raceway in Monterey in the circuit's third race, then reeled off a record six consecutive victories on his Honda, breaking Wayne Rainey's 1986 record of five straight. His sixth victory, at Sears Point Raceway in Sonoma, California, gave him the overall points lead ahead of Mike Hale, which he held by finishing second to Hale in the season's final event. Duhamel grew up in Quebec, Canada, and is the son of legendary road racer Yvon Duhamel of the 1970s. As a young boy, Miguel and his older brother Mario, another top road racer, would race minibikes in the basement of the family home. That introduction to two-wheel riding paid off in 1991 when Duhamel won his first road racing points title in the 600-cc **SuperSport** class. He won the SuperSport title twice more, in 1993 and 1995. Hale would have claimed the points title if not for Duhamel's amazing six-victory run, but he gladly accepted second place considering his violent accident at New Hampshire International Speedway. Hale lost control of his bike at the end of the race and slammed to the pavement at 130 miles per hour. He suffered a punctured and bruised lung, an injury he would aggravate later that year in another crash at the Suzuki Eight-Hour International event in Japan. But Hale was able to overcome such mishaps. It was an impressive season for a former dirt track racer from Texas who had entered his first Superbike contest just one year earlier.

No one has dominated the dirt track racing scene like Scott Parker. Scott was 14 years old when he won the 1976 AMA 250-cc Amateur National Dirt Track title. Two years

Canadian Miguel Duhamel earned the pole during qualifying for the 64th Daytona 200 on March 10, 2005, with a speed of 1 minute, 42.593 seconds on the 2.95 mile motorcycle circuit.

later he won the Junior National championship. He joined the Grand National Dirt Track Tour in 1979 and became the youngest winner at age 17 with a victory at the Du Quoin Mile in Illinois. Astride his modified Harley-Davidson, Parker Bubba stopped Shobert's run of points titles at three in 1988, and started a streak of his own by winning four in a row. He finished second to Chris Carr in 1992 and third to Carr and Ricky Graham in 1993 before rebounding to win his fifth crown the following year. That started a streak of five straight points titles. By 1999, Parker had racked up nine Grand National championships and 94 victories, more than twice as many as anyone else in history.

⑤
RIDING TODAY

The *Motocross des Nations* battles are still being waged. So are the Grand Prix championship events. But nowhere in the world is motorcycle racing as exciting as it is in the United States today. Road racing, dirt track racing, motocross, and Supercross are more popular in America now than ever before.

In 2004, AMA Superbike events averaged nearly 40,000 in attendance. All 10 races were broadcast live on television, and millions more watched the action. Meanwhile, interest in Supercross and motocross racing has gone through the roof. Fans pack outdoor stadiums and indoor arenas on a weekly basis to watch their racing heroes. What's more, motocross and Supercross events are televised by national sports network ESPN, with the races being broadcast to a huge worldwide audience in more than 70 countries.

With such high-level exposure, motorcycle manufacturers today offer riders lucrative contracts to join their "team" and race their machines. Another benefit for riders, of course, are the free motorcycles. Getting a free motorcycle certainly is a big deal to Superbike racers. Today's Superbikes are luxurious and powerful machines that cost more than the average car. Most machines are equipped with a 750-cc four-cylinder or 1000-cc twin-cylinder engine. With modifications, these high-performance bikes are capable of speeds approaching 200 miles an hour. Riders drag their knee within a fraction of an inch of the pavement while tearing through tight turns at more than 100 miles an hour. Crashes can be deadly despite all the protective gear drivers wear. Miguel Duhamel has crashed more than a dozen times in his career, yet he has somehow managed to remain in competition for 16 years. Duhamel is the all-time U.S. Superbike win list leader. In 2003, Duhamel earned his fourth AMA Superbike victory at Daytona International Speedway and made seven additional podium appearances in the series.

Innovations in dirt bikes have sent speeds rising in that sport as well. Racers power their machines around the one-mile oval course in dangerously tight bunches, flicking their bikes sideways into the turns, and then roaring down the straightaways at 130 miles per hour. The 750-cc twin-cylinder machines built by Harley-Davidson, Honda, and Ducati dominate the field.

While road racing and dirt track racing offer fans the spectacle of speed, motocross and Supercross racing provide an altogether different form of entertainment. The obstacle-filled courses pose as a challenge, both physical and mental, to the supremely athletic riders. Motocross courses that stretch across natural terrain are a grueling test for the racers, and it is not uncommon on a warm day for a rider to lose 10 pounds in an hour of racing. Supercross riders are acrobats on wheels. They perform airborne maneuvers that seem to defy the laws of gravity. Track builders often place three huge dirt jumps in a section covering as much as 80 feet, challenging riders to clear the last two jumps on the fly. And the riders respond. They accelerate into the first jump, and as

Ricky Carmichael appears to defy gravity as he launches his Honda over a jump at the Steel City Raceway in Delmont, Pennsylvania, on September 4, 2004. Carmichael went on to claim a second perfect racing season.

soon as they vault skyward, they leap up and pull their motorcycle upward with their legs, propelling themselves even higher than they normally would go. Obviously, the ability to land safely becomes an art in itself.

Ricky Carmichael answers reporters' questions after winning the 2004 AMA Chevrolet National Motocross Championship Series on August 22 in Binghamton, New York. It was an unprecedented fifth straight title, which Carmichael secured by winning all twelve races in the series.

Riders are well-compensated for their efforts. In 2004, through revenue generated mostly from sponsorships and gate receipts, racers competed on the AMA circuit for nearly $6 million in prize money and bonuses. A lot of that money went to Ricky Carmichael. The veteran racer from Havana,

Florida, claimed his unprecedented fifth straight AMA Chevrolet 250 Motocross points title in 2004. And he did it by winning all 12 races.

Only one other time did a racer go through an entire motocross season undefeated. It happened two years earlier when Carmichael himself did it. For Carmichael, the 2004 title was especially sweet because he was coming off a major injury that forced him to miss the 2004 Supercross campaign. He underwent graft surgery to replace a ligament in his knee after a horrible crash. "Everything about this year's championship was really special," Carmichael said. "My goal was to come back even stronger after my knee surgery."

For Carmichael, the 2004 title simply added to the most impressive racing resume in AMA motocross racing history. He burst onto the scene in 1996 to capture AMA Motocross/Supercross Rookie of the Year honors when he earned enough points for the award in just a single event. He then came into the 125-cc class and won three straight AMA National Motocross titles in addition to a 125 East Region Supercross title. In 2000, Carmichael moved up to the 250-cc class and began his current motocross points title streak. Along the way, he captured three AMA Supercross titles. Most impressive, Carmichael was the all-time wins leader in combined AMA motocross and Supercross victories with 107 victories entering 2005. And he hasn't let up on the throttle. Carmichael led through four of 20 laps in the 2005 Supercross series opener in Anaheim before crashing. He won the following week in Phoenix, Arizona. He won round three back in Anaheim. He won round four in San Francisco. In all, Carmichael won five straight races before Chad Reed broke the streak in San Diego. Reed surprised Carmichael by passing him on the final lap.

Chad Reed signals to the crowd after winning the 250-cc main event at the THQ AMA Supercross San Diego at Qualcomm Stadium, February 19, 2005. Reed broke Ricky Carmichael's 5-race winning streak when he passed Carmichael on the final lap. The Aussie is the first foreign-born racer to win the title in 13 years.

For Reed, the wise Australian rider who had recently moved to Dade City, Florida, finishing first had a familiar feel to it. Reed had capitalized on Carmichael's absence due to injury by winning the 2004 Supercross title. He became the first foreign-born rider to win the title in 13 years. Reed had won the opener in Anaheim and never looked back. He finished on the podium (in the top three) in every race. In the season's final race in Las Vegas, Nevada, Reed finished second behind Kevin Windham to secure the points title. "Winning this championship has been a life-long dream," said Reed. "I'm real happy to reach this goal. Nothing feels better than the first one. The fans have given me great support here in America and I really appreciate it."[6]

That same evening at Sam Boyd Stadium, James Stewart continued his dominance in the 125-cc class by winning the Dave Coombs Sr. 125 Shootout. At every level of competition since he was 10 years old, Stewart has been fastest on a motorcycle. He trained on the three practice tracks on 79 acres of property at his home in Haines City, Florida. Now at age 18, he was completing his streak of Supercross 125 victories. On the motocross circuit four months later, Stewart would tie Carmichael's mark of 26 victories in the 125 division in Binghamton, New York. A week later in Delmont, Pennsylvania, Stewart would win again for his 27th victory. He would close the season with his 28th and final victory for the record books. Stewart would move up to the 250 class in 2005. And he expected success. As the opener in Anaheim approached, Stewart was focused. "I've got one thing on my mind," he said. "Anaheim. I'm blocking out everything. Living for that moment."[7] Despite torrential rains on race day, Stewart proved he was ready. He recorded the fastest practice time of all the racers. Next, he won his **heat**. Finally, he finished fifth in the **main**. "It's funny because when most riders come into the 250 class it's cool even if they make the main and just have a decent race," Stewart said. "Now everyone is expecting me

James Stewart, right, of Haines City, Florida, celebrates his AMA Chevrolet 125-cc Motocross Championship win on May 30, 2004, by spraying champagne on Broc Hepler, who finished second. Stewart dominated the 125-cc class in 2004, and moved up to the 250 class in 2005.

to either win or crash my brains out."[8] Before Stewart could win, he crashed. The following week in Phoenix, Stewart posted the fastest practice time again. But on his last practice run, he lost control of his Kawasaki and slammed into the ground. He suffered a broken arm and missed the Supercross season.

Stewart would return in full force. But in the meantime, his absence did little to dim the glow cast by today's stars. Motocross and Supercross racers are becoming ever more popular, and they seem to be more skilled than ever before. Besides Carmichael, there are daredevils like Travis Pastrana, the wildly popular rider who has gained fame from Freestyle Motocross in the X Games. Kevin Windham and veteran Mike LaRocco are threats to win every time they race. And, of course, there is the return to competition of Jeremy McGrath. Even the star racers themselves know that they are just one in a galaxy of stars. "I'm honored to be mentioned as one of the top riders in this group," said Chad Reed, the defending Supercross champion, before the 2005 season. "If I weren't racing myself I would definitely be in the crowd watching."[9]

DID YOU KNOW?

Riding a motorcycle is dangerous. About 7 percent of all traffic deaths in the United States each year are motorcycle fatalities. Yet motorcycles are less than two percent of all vehicles on the road.* Why is riding a motorcycle so dangerous? The main reason, of course, is that there is little between the rider and the road. That is why it is important to wear proper protective gear.

The most important piece of safety equipment is the helmet. It is made of a hard outer shell, a visor to protect the face, and a special inner padding. Other safety equipment includes form-fitting gloves, special riding suits that do not rip easily, and sturdy high-top shoes or boots.

Racers also wear knee and elbow pads, as well as other safety gear. Smart riders are aware of the dangers of motorcycles and know how to dress to keep themselves safe.

*U.S. Department of Motor Vehicles, *www.dmv.state.va.us/ webdoc/general/safety/motorcycle/facts.asp.*

NOTES

Chapter 1

1. Jeremy McGrath, *Wide Open* (New York, NY: HarperCollins Publishers, Inc., 2004), 291–92.

2. "Reed Opens THQ AMA Supercross Series Title Defense in Anaheim, " January 3, 2005. *www.fastlaneracing.com/AMA/sx/010405a.html*.

3. Todd Harris, ESPN2 broadcast, February 6, 2005.

Chapter 3

4. McGrath, 175.

5. "Ricky Carmichael: 2004 AMA Chevrolet 250 Motocross Champion, " September 7, 2004. *www.transworldmotocross.com/mx/news/article/ 0, 13190, 693498, 00.html*.

Chapter 5

6. "Reed Wins First THQ AMA Supercross Crown, " May 3, 2004. *www.amamotocross.com/article.php? UID=mCXoOMiM0zosCjfV3P7N6TXtJ7mtG9&aid =3693*.

7. Chris Palmer, "Double Clutch, " *ESPN Magazine*.

8. Staff report, "Stars Truly Aligning in Anaheim, " January 4, 2005. *www.ESPN.com*.

9. Ibid.

CHRONOLOGY

1876 Nikolaus Otto builds internal combustion engine.

1885 Gottlieb Daimler designs two-wheeled machine.

1900 Albert Pope fits engine to a bike.

1901 William Harley and Arthur Davidson team up to build Harley-Davidson motorcycles.

1904 First International Cup Race run in France.

1907 First Tourist Trophy Race run on Isle of Man.

1908 Will Cook wins the first official motorcycle race at Brooklands, averaging 63 mph.

1911 Jake de Rosier uses the novel technique of slip-streaming to beat Charlie Collier.

1913 International Six-Days Trial begins.

1921 First European Grand Prix is held in Belgium.

1924 First officially sanctioned scrambles contest in Britain.

1931 AMA organizes first road races in the United States.

1937 First Daytona 200 is run.

1947 *Motocross des Nations* is founded.

1954 AMA establishes Grand National Dirt Track Series.

1961 Carroll Resweber wins his fourth consecutive Grand
Nationals Championship; first motorcycle races held
at Daytona International Speedway.

1967 Mike Hailwood wins his 11th Tourist Trophy Race,
breaking the longstanding mark of Stanley Woods;
Hailwood goes on to win a twelfth trophy.

1968 Cal Rayborn becomes first cyclist at Daytona to win
a race averaging over 100 mph.

1971 First official motocross held in the United States at
Daytona.

1972 First Supercross competition at Daytona; AMA
establishes National Championship Series for
motocross and Supercross.

1973 "Hurricane" Bob Hannah wins his third straight
championship.

1976 AMA creates Superbike Series.

1981 United States wins its first *Motocross des Nations*,
starting string of 13 victories.

1989 Bubba Shobert, a three-time Grand National Dirt
Track champion and one of the few also to win racing on asphalt, is nearly killed during a crash.

1993 Jeremy McGrath wins his first American
Motorcyclist Association Supercross
Championship—as a rookie.

1995 Scott Parker wins his record sixth Grand National points title.

1996 Jeremy McGrath wins his fourth straight AMA Supercross Championship, becoming, at age 24, the cyclist with the greatest number of AMA titles in history.

1999 Scott Parker wins his record 94th AMA Superbike race.

2000 Jeremy McGrath wins his record seventh Supercross title.

2002 Ricky Carmichael registers the first undefeated motocross season.

2004 Ricky Carmichael records his second undefeated motocross season.

James Stewart breaks Ricky Carmichael's record for 125-cc Supercross victories with a total of 28.

STATISTICS

AMA All-Time National Win Summary

250-cc Supercross

Jeremy McGrath, Encinitas, CA **72**

Ricky Carmichael, Havana, FL **33**

Rick Johnson, El Cajon, CA **28**

Bob Hannah, Whittier, CA **27**

Jeff Ward, Mission Viejo, CA **20**

Damon Bradshaw, Charlotte, NC **19**

250-cc Motocross

Ricky Carmichael, Havana, FL **49**

Bob Hannah, Whittier, CA **27**

Rick Johnson, El Cajon, CA **22**

Kent Howerton, San Antonio, TX **18**

Jeff Emig, Riverside, CA **16**

Jeremy McGrath, Encinitas, CA **15**

500-cc Motocross

Broc Glover, El Cajon, CA **19**

Brad Lackey, Pinole, CA **16**

Pierre Karsmakers, Holland **16**

David Bailey, Axton, VA **15**

Jeff Ward, San Juan Capistrano, CA **12**

Grand National Dirt Track Series

Scott Parker, Swartz Creek, MI **70**

Jay Springsteen, Lapeer, MI **41**

Ricky Graham, Salinas, CA **39**

Chris Carr, Valley Springs, CA **34**

Bubba Shobert, Lubbock, TX **33**

Superbike Road Racing

Fred Merkel, Stockton, CA **20**

Wayne Rainey, Downey, CA **16**

Freddie Spencer, Shreveport, LA **15**

Eddie Lawson, Upland, CA **14**

Doug Polen, Denton, TX **13**

GLOSSARY

American Motorcyclist Association: founded in 1924, the AMA is the world's largest motorsports governing body, overseeing more than 80 racing events in the United States.

Dabbing: In trials competition, an illegal move in which a rider momentarily touches his foot to the ground to maintain balance on his motorcycle.

Drag race: A short-distance race between two motorcycles in a straight line to see which is faster.

Enduro race: A long-distance race between a group of motorcycles across rugged terrain to test endurance.

Formula One: A form of motorcycle racing involving motorcycles using a certain high-powered fuel blend of gasoline, oil, and other power-boosting additives.

Four-stroke: A more complex engine than a two-stroke, in which a four-step cycle is used—intake, compression, power, and exhaust—to produce power.

Freestyle: A competition in which riders perform midair tricks to be scored by judges.

Hairpin: A sharp turn, 180 degrees or more, often shaped like a hairpin.

Heat: A qualifying race in which the top riders advance to the main race.

Holeshot: The point around the first turn where the track narrows and the order is established to begin the race.

Land speed record: The fastest recorded time in which a motorcycle is driven across a flat surface.

Main: The final race of the event, featuring the top 20 qualifying riders.

Motocross: A form of racing, usually involving small to mid-sized motorcycles, on an outdoor dirt track loop featuring jumps and sharp turns.

Podium: The stage on which the top three finishers of a race receive their awards.

Retirement: The withdrawal or removal from employment in a job; no longer working.

Rhythm section: A portion of the track with different-sized bumps.

Slipstreaming: A racing technique in which one motorcycle racer intentionally rides behind another in order to reduce wind resistance.

Superbike: Motorcycles with big engines, usually 600 cubic centimeters or more, used for racing on hard surfaces.

Supercross: A form of racing, usually involving small to mid-sized motorcycles, on an indoor arena dirt track loop featuring jumps and sharp turns.

SuperSport: A racing circuit, most popular in Europe, that features a series of hard track races involving motorcycles with big engines.

Transmission: The connection between the engine and the drive wheel that shifts gears, allowing the motorcycle to speed up or slow down.

Two-stroke: A simpler engine than a four-stroke, in which the spark plug fires every revolution.

Whoops: A series of small bumps; also called whoop-de-dos.

Yellow caution flag: A flag waved to indicate a serious hazard on or near the track; it tells drivers to proceed with caution.

FURTHER READING

Beyer, Mark. *Motorcycles of the Past*. New York, NY: PowerKids Press, 2005.

Drew, A.J. *The Everything Motorcycle Book*. Avon, MA: Adams Media Corporation, 2002.

Gibbs, Lynne. *Motorcycles*. North Mankato, MN: Chrysalis Education, 2003.

Graham, Ian. *Superbikes*. Chicago, IL: Heinemann Library, 2003.

Hendrickson, Steve. *Enduro Racing*. Mankato, MN: Capstone Press, 2000.

Hill, Lee Sullivan. *Motorcycles*. Minneapolis, MN: Lerner Publishing Group, 2004.

Kimber, David. *Motorcycle-Mania!* Milwaukee, WI: Gareth Stevens Publishing, 2004.

Sievert, Terri. *The World's Fastest Superbikes*. Mankato, MN: Capstone Press, 2002.

Stille, Darlene R. *Motorcycles*. Minneapolis, MN: Compass Point Books, 2004.

Tiner, John Hudson. *Motorcycles*. Mankato, MN: Creative Education, 2003.

BIBLIOGRAPHY

AMAMotocross.com. *www.amamotocross.com.*

ESPN.com. *http://espn.go.com.*

EXPN.com. *http://expn.go.com/expn/index.*

Fastlaneracing.com. *http://fastlaneracing.com.*

Graham, Ian. *Superbikes.* Chicago, IL: Heinemann Library, 2003.

McGrath, Jeremy. *Wide Open.* New York, NY: HarperCollins Publishers, Inc., 2004.

Savage, Jeff, *Motocross Cycles.* Mankato, MN: Capstone Press, 1996.

Savage, Jeff. *Supercross Motorcycle Racing.* Parsippany, NJ: Crestwood House, 1997.

Transworld Motocross. *www.transworldmotocross.com/mx.*

ADDRESSES

American Motorcyclist Association
13515 Yarmouth Drive
Pickerington, OH 43147

American Historic Racing Motorcycle Association
P.O. Box 1725
Goodlettsville, TN 37070

INTERNET SITES

www.ahrma.org

> *The home of the American Historic Racing Motorcycle Association (AHRAMA), this site is dedicated to enhancing the sport of historic motorcycle racing. The AHRMA is a chartered promoter of the American Motorcyclist Association and conducts amateur activities.*

www.ama-cycle.org

> *This is the site of the American Motorcyclist Association. Here you can find information and articles about the associaton and its events.*

www.amamotocross.com

> *This is the official site of the American Motorcyclist Associatin (AMA) Motocross Championship.*

www.expn.go.com/expn/index

> *EXPN.com is the site of the coverage of the X games.*

www.fastlaneracing.com

> *Fastlaneracing.com provides links to O'Reilly American Sprint Car Series National Tour (ASCS) and AMADirect. These sites publish articles about racing.*

www.motorcycles.about.com

> *This site gives information about motorcycles, with information about make, model, and use of various types of motorcycles.*

www.sports.espn.go.com/rpm/index

> *ESPN.com is the site of many different sports. This specific page will direct you to ESPNs coverage of motor sports.*

www.sportnetwork.net/main/s180.htm

> *Motorcycle Racing Online is the site of unofficial motorcycle racing online news and views.*

www.transworldmotocross.com/ms

> *Transworld Motocross gives information on motocross mews, race reports, videos, photos, interviews, and how-tos for motocross racing.*

INDEX

ABOUT THE AUTHOR

Jeff Savage began his motorcycle career on the dusty logging roads of Cow Creek, California. His career ended there as well. He is the award-winning author of over 150 books for children. Jeff lives in the Napa Valley with his wife, Nancy, and sons, Taylor and Bailey. You can visit his website at *www.jeffsavage.com.*